One Red Tomato Counting to Twenty

Un Tomate Rojo Contando Hasta Veinte

Karen Pilman Soren Pilman

For Lennon, Eliott,
Elin,
Rudy and Anders

One   Uno

One tomato
counting to twenty.

**Un tomate
contando hasta veinte.**

1 2 3 4 5
6 7 8 9 10
11 12 13 14 15
16 17 18 19 20

Two   Dos

Two tomatoes
sailing in a boat.

**Dos tomates
navegando en un bote.**

Three   Tres

Three tomatoes
playing baseball.

**Tres tomates
jugando béisbol.**

Four tomatoes
swinging on swings.

**Cuatro tomates columpiándose
en columpios.**

Five   Cinco

Five tomatoes reading books on the floor.

Cinco tomates leyendo libros en el suelo.

Six Seis

Six tomatoes
hanging upside down.

Seis tomates
colgándose boca abajo.

Seven   Siete

Seven tomatoes
sitting in a window.

**Siete tomates
sentados en una ventana.**

Eight   Ocho

Eight tomatoes
making pizza.

**Ocho tomates
haciendo pizza.**

Nine   Nueve

Nine tomatoes
running a race.

**Nueve tomates
corriendo una carrera.**

Ten   Diez

Ten tomatoes
fishing off the dock.

**Diez tomates
pescando en el muelle.**

Eleven   Once

Eleven tomatoes playing soccer.

Once tomates jugando fútbol.

Twelve   Doce

Twelve tomatoes
relaxing at the beach.

Doce tomates
relajándose en la playa.

Thirteen   Trece

Thirteen tomatoes
playing instruments.

**Trece tomates
tocando instrumentos.**

Fourteen   Catorce

Fourteen tomatoes celebrating a birthday party.

Catorce tomates celebrando una fiesta de cumpleaños.

Fifteen tomatoes learning in school.

Quince tomates aprendiendo en la escuela.

Sixteen tomatoes
riding on a bus.

Dieciséis tomates
montados en un autobús.

Seventeen Diecisiete

Seventeen tomatoes
flying kites.

**Diecisiete tomates
volando cometas.**

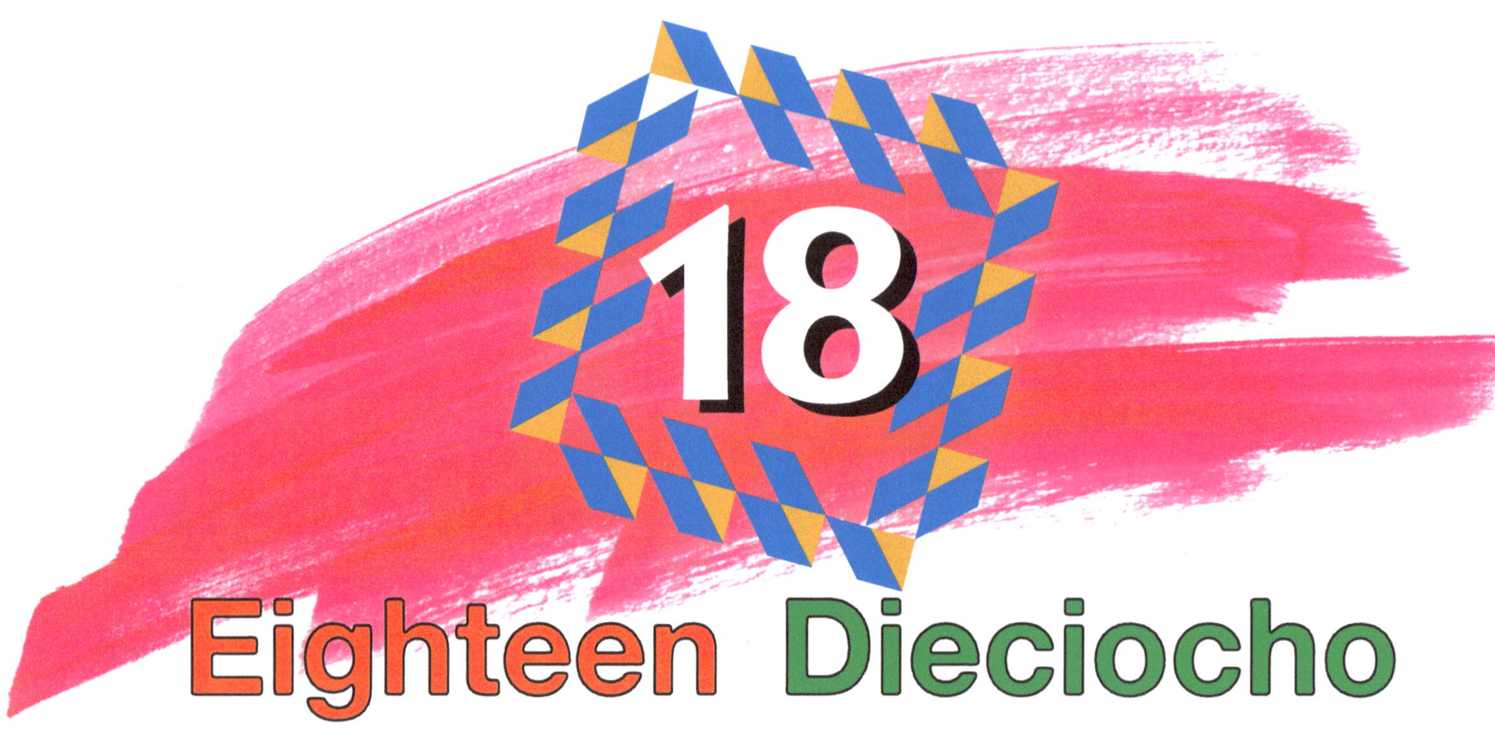

Eighteen Dieciocho

Eighteen tomatoes rolling down a hill.

Dieciocho tomates rodando por una colina.

Nineteen Diecinueve

Nineteen tomatoes
singing a song.

**Diecinueve tomates
cantando una canción.**

Twenty   Veinte

Twenty tomatoes
sleeping on the floor.

**Veinte tomates
durmiendo en el suelo.**

www.ingramcontent.com/pod-product-compliance
Lightning Source LLC
Chambersburg PA
CBHW042123030726
47599CB00002B/324